Original title:
Frosted Dreams

Copyright © 2024 Swan Charm
All rights reserved.

Author: Liisi Lendorav
ISBN HARDBACK: 978-9916-79-780-8
ISBN PAPERBACK: 978-9916-79-781-5
ISBN EBOOK: 978-9916-79-782-2

The Lull of Winter's Breath

In the hush of silver night,
Snowflakes dance, oh what a sight.
Trees wear blankets, soft and white,
Whispers echo, pure delight.

Icicles hang like chandeliers,
Laughter fades, but joy adheres.
Nature rests, shedding its fears,
Winter's lull, a song that cheers.

Fires crackle, warmth draws near,
Shadows flicker, moments dear.
Cocoa sips, we hold them near,
In this season, hearts sincere.

Frosted windows, tales unfold,
Stories shared, memories old.
Time stands still, as night grows cold,
In winter's breath, a magic bold.

As dawn arrives with golden hue,
The world awakens, fresh and new.
Winter fades, yet dreams hold true,
In every heart, a spark imbued.

Shadows Play on Crystal Fields

In fields where shadows dance and sway,
The crystal glimmers in the play.
Each whispering breeze brings forth a sigh,
As dusk descends, the stars will fly.

Light flickers soft upon the ground,
In patterns lost but deeply found.
The day retreats, a gentle fade,
While shadows bloom in twilight's shade.

Here, dreams inhabit every space,
A fleeting glimpse, a soft embrace.
Nature's canvas wide and free,
As night unveils its mystery.

Echoes linger, soft and light,
In the calm of approaching night.
These crystal fields, a sacred home,
Where shadows dance and spirits roam.

Shards of Light in a Frozen World

In frozen realms where silence reigns,
Shards of light break winter's chains.
Each glimmer speaks of warmth untold,
A promise wrapped in threads of gold.

Beneath the frost, a heartbeat lies,
Awakening with the morning skies.
Each sparkle tells a tale so bright,
Of hope reborn in purest light.

The bitter chill cannot confine,
The beauty found in nature's design.
For in the cold, the spirit thrives,
And through the ice, the soul survives.

As twilight drapes its velvet veil,
The shards of light begin to pale.
Yet in the heart, the warmth will stay,
A beacon through the longest day.

A Tapestry of Ice and Memory

With threads of ice and whispers old,
A tapestry of tales unfolds.
Each crystal stitch holds memories near,
Of seasons past and moments dear.

In patterns woven through the years,
A dance of joy, a trace of tears.
The chilling echoes softly call,
Reminding us we rise, we fall.

Beneath the surface, stories hide,
In frozen locks where dreams abide.
The fabric sways with winds of time,
An art of life, a silent rhyme.

As layers shift and seasons change,
The tapestry begins to rearrange.
Yet through it all, we find our way,
In ice-bound threads of yesterday.

Ephemeral Glories of the Frost

In morning light, the frost does gleam,
A fleeting touch, a whispered dream.
Each crystal flake, a moment brief,
A fragile bloom, yet full of belief.

As time slips by, the beauty fades,
Yet still it holds, in light it wades.
A transient glow beneath the sun,
Ephemeral glories just begun.

The world adorned in silver lace,
A winter's kiss, a soft embrace.
With every breath, the cold does bite,
Yet warms the heart with pure delight.

As shadows stretch with setting sun,
The dance of frost has just begun.
For in its chill, we come alive,
In fleeting moments, we survive.

Whispers in the White Silence

In the hush of falling snow,
Dreams weave softly, lost and slow.
Frosted whispers fill the air,
Silent secrets everywhere.

Moonlight dances on the ground,
Each step echoes, soft and round.
Nature's breath, a gentle sigh,
Underneath the starry sky.

Branches bend with icy grace,
Time stands still in this embrace.
Heartbeats mingle, calm and free,
In the white, pure tapestry.

Shadows flicker, spirits play,
Guided by the light of day.
In this quiet, all is calm,
Winter's touch, a soothing balm.

The world wrapped in silver white,
Whispers call through endless night.
Here in silence, fears take flight,
Lost in dreams till morning light.

Charmed by the Cold

Frosty breath beneath the frost,
In the chill, we count the cost.
Eyes like diamonds, bright and bold,
Hearts entwined, we're charmed by cold.

Snowflakes dance on whispered dreams,
Life ignites with frozen themes.
In the stillness, warmth is found,
Softened by the winter sound.

Bare trees stand like ancient guards,
Holding silence like a bard's.
Charming tales of love's embrace,
In the cold, we find our place.

Memories wrapped in icy lace,
Each moment holds a sacred space.
In the dark, your hand in mine,
Charmed by cold, our hearts align.

Beneath the stars, we share a smile,
Every heartbeat, worth the while.
In the frost, our spirits soar,
Charmed by cold, forevermore.

Beneath the Icy Canopy

Beneath the boughs of frosty trees,
Whispers float upon the breeze.
Icicles hang like crystal tears,
Winter's beauty calms our fears.

Footfalls muffled in the snow,
Secrets wrapped in soft hello.
Nature cradles hopes anew,
In this world, a tranquil view.

Stars peep through the icy veil,
Glimmering like a silver trail.
Magic lingers, time stands still,
Dreams awaken, hearts will fill.

Shadows stretch as daylight fades,
Winter's chill in twilight's shades.
Underneath this snowy dome,
Found in nature, we are home.

Each branch bows with weighty grace,
In this quiet, we find our place.
Beneath the canopy so wide,
Winter's wonder, our warm guide.

Secrets of the Winter Night

A hush falls over land and sea,
Winter's night, a mystery.
Stars align in twinkling grace,
Secrets held in cold embrace.

Fires crackle, shadows cast,
Moments cherished, joys amassed.
In the dark, our laughter sings,
A celebration winter brings.

Moonlit paths and icy streams,
Frosty dreams wrapped in moonbeams.
Whispers shared in quiet tones,
In the night, we're not alone.

Ski tracks lead to places bold,
Stories waiting to be told.
Touch the frost, feel the delight,
Embrace the secrets of the night.

Each breath fogs a chilly air,
Every moment holds a prayer.
In this silence, hopes take flight,
Found forever in winter's light.

Winter's Reverie

Softly falls the winter snow,
Whispers in the evening glow.
Blankets white on earth's embrace,
Time slows down in quiet grace.

Frosted trees with limbs aglow,
Silence deep as shadows grow.
Dreams of warmth within the chill,
Heartbeats echo, calm and still.

Candles flicker, shadows dance,
Moments held in knowing glance.
Winter's breath a gentle sigh,
Memories that never die.

Footsteps crunch on frozen ground,
Nature's beauty all around.
In this world of purest white,
Magic glimmers in the night.

As the stars begin to gleam,
Awakening a whispered dream.
Winter's canvas, vast and wide,
Hope resides where dreams abide.

Glacial Aspirations

Mountains rise with icy pride,
In their shadows dreams reside.
Crystals gleam in morning light,
Glacial hopes take airy flight.

Rivers freeze, a silent dance,
Nature grants a fleeting chance.
Underneath the winter sky,
Aspirations learn to fly.

Snowflakes drift on gentle breeze,
Whispers float through winter trees.
In their fall, a promise made,
In the cold, ambitions laid.

Echoes of a future bright,
Find their voice in still of night.
Stars align, the universe spins,
Where the silence of hope begins.

Through the ice, a spark ignites,
Guiding dreams to soaring heights.
In the chill, our hearts still burn,
For glacial hopes, we yearn and learn.

Snow-kissed Hopes

Beneath the moon's soft, silver sheen,
Snowflakes fall, a tranquil scene.
Blankets hug the sleeping ground,
In this hush, our dreams are found.

Footprints lead to secret places,
Where snow-kissed love embraces faces.
Whispers carried on the air,
Hopes rising, light as a prayer.

Glistening under starlit skies,
Each small flake, a sweet surprise.
In the cold, we find our light,
Guided through the peaceful night.

Shadows dance in candle's glow,
Warmth within the winter's flow.
Snow-kissed wishes softly bloom,
In the heart, dispel the gloom.

As dawn breaks on winter's breath,
Hope renews beyond the death.
In the winter's frosty hold,
Every dream is purest gold.

Frigid Musings

In the stillness, thoughts arise,
Frigid musings touch the skies.
Chill of air through branches weaves,
Stories whispered by the leaves.

Frosted glass with swirling lines,
Nature paints its secret signs.
In the quiet, hearts align,
Moments shared are pure, divine.

Winter nights, a world transformed,
Wrapped in blankets, thoughts warmed.
Each soft breath like winter air,
In these musings, find our care.

Trees stand tall, their limbs adorned,
With glints of ice, our hearts are warmed.
Frigid winds may chill our bones,
But in our dreams, we find our homes.

In the dance of frozen light,
Hope emerges from the night.
Frigid musings hold the key,
Unlocking what we long to see.

Glistening Reflections of Tomorrow

In the dawn's gentle light,
Dreams begin to arise,
Mirrored in puddles bright,
Hope dances in the skies.

Pavements shimmer and glow,
Each step a new refrain,
With every breath, we sow,
A future free of pain.

The world is vast and wide,
With horizons yet unseen,
In stillness, hearts collide,
Unraveling the serene.

Pretty visions we hold,
Within our vibrant minds,
Stories yet to be told,
In every heart, love binds.

Tomorrow's light shines clear,
As we walk hand in hand,
With whispers we hold dear,
In this enchanted land.

A Palette of Winter Whispers

Snowflakes swirl and glisten,
Crafting a dreamlike scene,
In silence, they do listen,
To secrets softly glean.

The trees wear coats of white,
Branches bowed low with grace,
In the hush of night,
Nature finds its embrace.

Frosted breaths drift and sway,
Like whispers from the past,
Each moment slips away,
In this beauty, we're cast.

A canvas cold and pure,
Painted in shades of frost,
In winter's heart, we're sure,
Of warmth found in the lost.

With laughter, we create,
Joy in every snowy flake,
Together, we await,
What the thaw shall remake.

Snowbound Fables of the Heart

Through the drifts, we wander,
With stories to unfold,
In the silence, we ponder,
As the night grows bold.

The moon bathes all in light,
Casting shadows, soft and long,
In the cold, hearts ignite,
Finding where we belong.

Each snowdrift holds a tale,
Of dreams that danced and played,
In this winter's pale,
Old memories never fade.

Fables whisper in the breeze,
Of love and dreams once spun,
Woven through the frigid trees,
Tales of hearts that won.

Together we'll embrace,
The magic of this night,
In snowbound, warm space,
Our love shines ever bright.

The Beauty of a Chilling Whisper

In whispers soft and low,
The winter breeze does sigh,
Caressing the ground below,
A gentle lullaby.

Textures crisp and clear,
Snowflakes kiss my cheek,
Each breath a frosty sphere,
In chill, the heart feels meek.

Yet beauty blossoms bright,
In shadows, layers deep,
With every frosty bite,
The world wakes from its sleep.

Echoes of serene grace,
In a landscape fresh and white,
In the moon's warm embrace,
All fears vanish from sight.

As we share this night,
With chill wrapped in our hearts,
Together, spirits light,
In quiet, love imparts.

Veils of Crystal Dreams

In a world of whispers soft,
Veils of crystal dance above,
Illusions dream in twilight's glow,
Carried by the winds of love.

Silken threads weave tales untold,
Beneath the moon's enchanting light,
Faces hidden in shadows deep,
Wandering through the velvet night.

Stars blink gently, secrets shared,
Mirrors of the heart's delight,
Each breath a promise, delicate,
Caught in the web of silver-white.

Echoes linger, soft and light,
Holding dreams in fragile hands,
With every heartbeat, they ignite,
A symphony of timeless strands.

Veils of crystal drift and sigh,
A tapestry of hopes and schemes,
Beneath the vast, embracing sky,
We whisper softly, lost in dreams.

Waltz of the Winter Spirits

Snowflakes twirl in silent grace,
Winter spirits spin and sway,
A dance upon the frozen ground,
Where shadows play in shades of gray.

Pine trees wear their coats of white,
While frosty breath fills the air,
Echos of laughter, soft and bright,
Whispering tales without a care.

Moonlight glimmers on crisp snow,
Casting magic in each drape,
As spirits join the waltz below,
In rhythmic steps, a dance they shape.

Glowing embers warm the night,
Fires crackle, stories blend,
Beneath the stars, spirits take flight,
In winter's embrace, they find a friend.

Through the chill, the heart beats warm,
As footsteps mingle, soft and slow,
In the memory of quiet charm,
The winter spirits put on a show.

Silhouettes in the Frosty Glow

Underneath the pale moonlight,
Silhouettes begin to dance,
Wrapped in whispers of the night,
Caught in winter's fleeting chance.

Trees stand tall, their branches bare,
Against the sky of endless blue,
Shadows cast with tender care,
Painting dreams in frosty hue.

Footsteps echo, soft and low,
Carving paths in crisp, white snow,
Hearts entwined in gentle flow,
Where the peaceful moments grow.

As the chill nips at my nose,
Laughter rings in the stillness near,
Each exhaled breath, a fleeting rose,
Moments cherished, warm and clear.

In the frost, our spirits blend,
Together 'neath the silver glow,
Holding on until the end,
In silhouettes of love, we grow.

Serene Reflections Beneath Stars

Quiet whispers fill the air,
Serene reflections, calm and bright,
Stars adorn the velvet night,
As dreams take flight without a care.

Rippling waters catch the light,
Mirrors glinting, framed in dark,
With every flicker, memories spark,
In the stillness of the night.

Beneath the vast celestial show,
Hearts align with gentle grace,
Each star a friend, in this embrace,
Guiding hearts where rivers flow.

Softly drifting, thoughts arise,
In the cradle of the earth,
Echoing laughter, tales of worth,
Boundless dreams beneath the skies.

With each moment, time stands still,
Wrapped in shadows, bright and far,
Here, we fill our hearts with will,
In serene reflections, true as stars.

Frosty Impressions

Morning light breaks through the frost,
Whispers of cold where warmth is lost.
Trees adorned in icy lace,
Nature's quiet, frozen grace.

Footprints trail on glistening white,
Each step a dance in winter's night.
Breath forms clouds in frosty air,
Moments hang, fragile and rare.

Snowflakes tumble, soft and slow,
A symphony of flurries below.
Stillness reigns, the world in pause,
In this chill, a magic draws.

Icicles gleam like crystal spears,
Reflecting light, dispelling fears.
The world transformed in winter's clutch,
A frosty spell, a gentle touch.

As evening falls, stars appear bright,
Guiding dreams through the quiet night.
In this calm, hope feels near,
Frosty impressions, warm and clear.

Winter's Palette

Canvas of white, a snowy greet,
Colors of winter at our feet.
Brushstrokes sweeping across the land,
Nature's art, forever grand.

Shades of blue in the twilight sky,
Dusk descends with a gentle sigh.
Branches dressed in silver sheen,
A breathtaking view, serene and clean.

Orange glow from homes within,
Inviting warmth against the chill's spin.
Footprints wander, stories unfold,
Tales of warmth in the bitter cold.

Soft whispers echo through the trees,
Carried by the chill of frigid breeze.
Each moment painted with gentle care,
Winter's palette, beyond compare.

As night draws close, the stars ignite,
A tapestry woven, pure delight.
In this season, we find solace true,
Winter's colors, a vibrant view.

Dazzling Dreams

Under the stars, dreams take flight,
Whispers of magic in the night.
Snowflakes dance as if in trance,
Each twirl a dream, a fleeting chance.

Sparkling lights on branches glow,
A serene hush, beneath the snow.
Imagination swirls and sings,
In winter's grasp, enchanting things.

Frosted windows tell a tale,
Of journeys great, of love's soft trail.
Each shadow cast upon the ground,
In dazzling dreams, our hearts are found.

Moonlight drapes a silver shawl,
As we embrace the night's sweet call.
In quiet moments, dreams we chase,
A world transformed, a sacred space.

With morning light, dreams fade away,
Yet in our hearts, they still will stay.
Dazzling whispers of hope and cheer,
Fueling our souls throughout the year.

Silvery Enigma

Veils of frost cover the ground,
Where secrets of winter can be found.
In the hush, a story looms,
Nature wrapped in silver blooms.

Mysterious shadows dance and play,
As twilight fades to close the day.
Footsteps echo, soft yet clear,
In the enigma, we draw near.

Branches weave a tangled design,
In the stillness, our hearts align.
A riddle carved in frost and ice,
Holding wonders that entice.

Moonlit paths that twist and turn,
In each moment, we brightly yearn.
The night unfolds, a precious gem,
In this silvery realm, we blend.

As morning dawns, the light reveals,
The beauty that winter conceals.
A silvery enigma, whispers gleam,
In every breath, we dare to dream.

Glimmers of a Shimmering Past

In twilight's soft and gentle glow,
Faded memories start to show.
Whispers dart like fireflies,
Illuminating silent sighs.

Old photographs in frames so worn,
Echo tales of loves once sworn.
Each glance brings a tender ache,
As time's current starts to wake.

Beneath the oak where shadows dance,
Time stands still, lost in a trance.
Leaves of gold in autumn's breath,
Speak of life, and love, and death.

Dreams woven with strands of gold,
Stories shared, both new and old.
Glimmers from the heart's deep well,
In their warmth, we long to dwell.

Embers fade but never cease,
In memories, we find our peace.
Each shimmer holds a precious key,
To unlock the past, eternally.

Dreams Wrapped in Glistening Layers

In night's embrace, the stars conspire,
To weave our dreams of softest fire.
Wrapped in whispers, time entwines,
Each layer formed from secret signs.

Silken threads of hope and night,
Glistening under moonlit light.
A tapestry of wishes made,
In quiet hearts, where dreams cascade.

Clouds that drift like gentle sighs,
Carrying hopes across the skies.
With every dawn, a journey starts,
In layers deep, we guard our hearts.

Moments caught in silken webs,
Traces of what the heart forgets.
In each layer, stories blend,
As we find the path to mend.

Wrapped in dreams, forever free,
Beyond the reach of time's decree.
Glistening layers, soul's delight,
Guide us gently through the night.

The Art of Winter's Embrace

Snowflakes dance like silent sighs,
Painting white on midnight skies.
Each breath forms clouds, soft and light,
In winter's arms, we hold the night.

Frost-kissed branches, a crystal lace,
Nature's touch in an icy embrace.
While the world sleeps, hushed and still,
Winter whispers without a thrill.

Footprints lace the blanket white,
A journey started in the night.
Every step a story told,
In the frigid grasp, our hearts are bold.

Softly gliding through frozen scenes,
We find joy in winter's dreams.
Glistening landscapes, serene and vast,
Nature's canvas, a spell that's cast.

In the cold, we find our peace,
Winter's art brings sweet release.
A fleeting moment, pure and bright,
In winter's arms, we feel the light.

Crystal Visions in the Stillness

In quiet hours before the dawn,
Crystal visions linger on.
Reflections dance on water's face,
Echoing time, a moment's grace.

Gentle ripples, soft and slow,
Waves of silence ebb and flow.
Nature's secrets softly spill,
In stillness found, a heart to fill.

Moonlight bathes the world in dreams,
Lighting paths with silver beams.
Each whisper of the night's calm air,
Holds the beauty we all share.

Frozen moments captured tight,
In crystal visions, pure delight.
Every glance a story spins,
In the stillness, hope begins.

With every breath, we touch the past,
In visions bright, our hearts held fast.
Through the stillness, we can see,
Life's reflections, wild and free.

Silvered Nightmares

In the silence of darkened dreams,
Whispers float on moonlit beams.
Shadows dance with a haunting grace,
Silvered fears in a twilight lace.

Eyes that glimmer, lost in fright,
Caught between the day and night.
Winds that sigh like a mourning dove,
Silvered nightmares, devoid of love.

Through the mist where phantoms play,
Echoes linger, fading away.
Shattered hopes like glass on ground,
In this realm, no peace is found.

A chilling touch, a ghostly glance,
In the shadows, lost in trance.
Yet deep within, a spark remains,
Silvered nightmares, endless chains.

Glinting Shadows

Beneath the break of dawning light,
Echoes stir, both soft and slight.
Glinting shadows stretch and yawn,
Chasing dreams from dusk till dawn.

Flickers fade and then arise,
In the corners of our eyes.
Silent whispers weave and weave,
Glinting shadows as they deceive.

Hopes entwined in midnight's fold,
Stories of the brave and bold.
As the stars begin to glow,
Glinting shadows start to show.

Tales of old in the twilight spread,
In the dances of the dead.
Yet in darkness, some still gleam,
Fleeting moments, chasing dreams.

Dreamscapes of Ice

In a world where crystals shine,
Frozen thoughts on a silver line.
Whispers woven in frosty breath,
Dreamscapes of ice, a dance with death.

Each step echoes, soft and slow,
Through a landscape where cold winds blow.
Beneath the stars, a glacial sea,
Dreamscapes of ice, calling to me.

Reflections trapped in the frozen tide,
Hopes encased where shadows hide.
Yet in this crystal vale, I find,
The warmth of dreams, a longing mind.

Even in frost, there's beauty too,
In every flake that sparkles anew.
Dreamscapes of ice, a chilly embrace,
Holding secrets in a white lace.

Lunar Glaze

Underneath the silver moon,
Softly hums a haunting tune.
Lunar glaze on tranquil seas,
Whispers echo with the breeze.

Night unfurls her velvet cloak,
Stars align with every stroke.
In the silence, dreams take flight,
Beneath the peace of gentle night.

Glowing paths where shadows creep,
In the quiet, secrets seep.
Lunar glaze on tender skin,
Awakens places deep within.

With each breath, the night grows old,
Tales of wonder, softly told.
Beneath the moon, our souls ignite,
In the shimmer of starry light.

Lattice of Light in the Darkness

In shadows deep, a glow appears,
Flickering softly, banishing fears.
Threads of hope weave through the night,
A lattice formed, a dance of light.

Stars whisper secrets, ancient and bright,
Guiding lost souls towards what feels right.
In the void, a gentle embrace,
A tapestry brightens, filling the space.

Where darkness looms, warmth draws near,
Light's delicate touch, soothing and clear.
With every pulse, the heart ignites,
A beacon of dreams in endless nights.

In the silence, a promise hums,
Resilient hope, a heartbeat drums.
A lattice of strength, woven in trust,
In the darkness, we rise from the dust.

The Quiet Symphony of Snowflakes

Falling gently, soft as a dream,
Each snowflake dances, a silent gleam.
Whispers of winter, pure and serene,
Nature's lullaby, a peaceful scene.

They twirl and swirl with graceful ease,
Kissing the earth, a soft-woven fleece.
In the hush of night, they sing their song,
A quiet symphony, where we belong.

Sparkling jewels on branches cling,
Cloaks the world in a shimmering ring.
Footprints fade in a glistening hue,
Wrapped in silence, the night feels new.

Each flake a story, unique in form,
Together they blanket, quiet and warm.
In winter's embrace, hearts come alive,
To the symphony's rhythm, we all strive.

Glazed Horizons at Dusk

As the sun bows low, worlds collide,
Colors of grace on the evening tide.
A canvas brushed with hues so bold,
Whispers of twilight, stories untold.

Beyond the hills, the sky ablaze,
In softest whispers, we lose our gaze.
Golden threads weave through the mist,
In the fading light, moments persist.

Shadows lengthen, embrace the plight,
Echoing dreams in the hush of night.
With every heartbeat, reality fades,
In the glazed horizons, magic cascades.

A gentle reminder, beauty withstands,
In dusk's embrace, hope expands.
As day sighs goodbye, stars take their place,
The dance of dusk, a warm embrace.

Ethereal Ballet of Ice

In crystalline realms, where whispers glide,
An ethereal ballet, where soft dreams hide.
Each flake a dancer, a delicate form,
Twisting and turning, they weather the storm.

Beneath the moon's watch, they gracefully play,
In the still of the night, they drift and sway.
A world frozen still, yet alive with grace,
An odyssey written in time and space.

Glistening jewels on branches unfold,
Tales of the winter, ancient and bold.
As shadows mingle, they form a show,
An ethereal beauty, with every flow.

In silence they twirl, in harmony they freeze,
Echoing soft notes that dance in the breeze.
The ballet of ice, a transient phase,
Where time seems to shimmer in winter's gaze.

Whispering Flurries

Softly the snowflakes dance down,
Whispers of winter in a swirling gown.
They cover the ground with a silvery light,
A delicate hush in the heart of the night.

Silent the world in a blanket of white,
All worries fading, wrapped up tight.
Each flake a story, a moment in time,
Whispering softly in verses of rhyme.

Trees wear their coats of frost-kissed grace,
Nature's own beauty, a tranquil embrace.
With every flurry, the silence grows deep,
In this winter's magic, my heart learns to leap.

Footsteps are muffled on soft snowy ground,
A memory born where love may be found.
Each breath a cloud in the crisp, frozen air,
Whispering secrets, we're free without care.

As day breaks gently, a soft glow appears,
The sun greets the land, chasing away fears.
With whispers of flurries now fading from sight,
Winter's sweet promise will linger tonight.

Frostbite Serenade

Under the moon's tender gaze,
Frozen whispers weave their maze.
Chilling notes in the frosty air,
A serenade, soft as a prayer.

Crystals glisten with delicate grace,
Nature's jewels, in a wintry embrace.
Every breeze carries a song,
In the silence, memories belong.

Hearts wrapped warm in layers of hope,
Treading through snow, we learn to cope.
The frostbite's kiss, a gentle sting,
But love's warm glow is a powerful thing.

Stars overhead twinkle bright,
Illuminating the soft, silent night.
In the quiet, there's magic so rare,
Whispers of frost in the crisp, clean air.

Notes of the night in a chilly embrace,
The song of the frost, a timeless trace.
As the dawn breaks, the symphony fades,
Yet in our hearts, that serenade stays.

Frosted Echoes

Echoes of winter drift through the trees,
Soft as the breath of a gentle breeze.
Each flake that falls, a story untold,
Whispers of magic in shimmer and gold.

Footsteps crunch on a blanket of white,
As shadow and light play in the night.
Frozen reflections in a silvery stream,
The world holds its breath, lost in a dream.

Under the stars in this vast, quiet space,
Nature sings sweetly, a lullaby's grace.
The echoes of frost brush against my skin,
In this cherished moment, we all can begin.

With every shimmer, a new tale is spun,
Frosted echoes, the dance of the sun.
In the heart of the winter, we find delight,
In the whispers that linger, soft, pure, and bright.

So let us embrace this frosted refrain,
A melody woven in joy and pain.
For in every echo, a memory gleams,
Like the frost on the window, alive in our dreams.

Ethereal Crystals

Delicate diamonds on a morning walk,
Crystals of frost in a sweet, silent talk.
The world is adorned in a shimmering gown,
Each step feels lighter as snow swirls down.

Whispers of magic in each glistening hue,
Nature's own artwork, each moment feels new.
The air is crisp, and the sunlight brings cheer,
Ethereal crystals drawing us near.

Branches bend gently under winter's sweet load,
As shadows and light create patterns bestowed.
With every breath, there's a softness that lingers,
In our fingertips, we feel nature's fingers.

Moments like these, oh how they inspire,
Warmth in our hearts, igniting a fire.
The crunch of the snow beneath our warm feet,
Each ethereal crystal our spirits will greet.

So here's to the beauty in winter's embrace,
To the joy and the wonder of nature's grace.
With ethereal crystals, let's find our true way,
In the dance of the snow, let our hearts play.

Reflections in a Silver Lake

In the morning light, it gleams,
A mirror of dreams, so calm and deep.
Whispers of the trees, it seems,
Hold secrets the waters keep.

Birds glide above in graceful arcs,
Their shadows dance on glistening skin.
Nature's canvas, painted sparks,
Where day and night softly begin.

Lily pads float, a gentle sway,
The world's reflections, a soft embrace.
Ripples weave through the light of day,
Each moment cherished, a quiet grace.

The sun retreats, the colors blend,
Gold and purple kiss the sky.
In stillness, we find a friend,
In silvered waters, we learn to fly.

Stars twinkle softly, a nighttime show,
Guiding lost wishes to distant shores.
In this moment, time moves slow,
In reflections, we find open doors.

The Breath of Frozen Fantasies

Cold winds whisper through moonlit trees,
Enchanting dreams in the frosty air.
Every flake, a tale, it frees,
Creating wonders beyond compare.

Footprints trace paths on shimmering white,
A garden of icicles, all aglow.
In the stillness, magic takes flight,
Where hopes wander, and spirits grow.

Every breath, a cloud, soft and bright,
In the silence, we lose all our fears.
Frozen fantasies dance in the night,
Transforming each moment into years.

Snowflakes cradle the velvet ground,
While stars twinkle in cosmic cheer.
In this realm, joy can be found,
As frost-kissed visions draw ever near.

With hearts aglow, we chase the dream,
In this winter's embrace, we trust.
The breath of cold's a gentle gleam,
Connecting us, like love, to dust.

Sparkling Thoughts on Silent Nights

Under the blanket of velvet skies,
Stars sprinkle wishes as dreams take flight.
In hushed moments where silence lies,
Thoughts shimmer softly, pure and bright.

Whispers of wind through branches play,
Caressing the world in tender grace.
Memories twinkle like a grand ballet,
Dance of the past in this sacred space.

Moonlight bathes the earth in peace,
As shadows stretch and softly sigh.
In this stillness, worries cease,
Nature's lullaby, a gentle sigh.

Beneath the glow, our hearts align,
With every spark, a story told.
In the stillness, our souls entwine,
As we surrender to moments bold.

On sparkling nights, magic reveals,
A tapestry woven of dreams and light.
In silence, the universe feels,
A connection profound on this starry night.

Beneath the Surface of Snow

Layers of white cloak the world below,
A silent blanket over dreams untold.
Whispers of secrets the wind may know,
Wrapped in a silence, peaceful and cold.

Footprints mark journeys, not far away,
As nature hides all its vibrant hues.
Underneath, life waits for spring's ballet,
A symphony of colors, fresh and new.

Icicles hang from eaves like glass,
Each drip a memory of water's play.
Beneath the surface, a life will pass,
While winter cradles the green away.

In twilight's grasp, shadows softly blend,
Secret stories weave through the night.
Beneath it all, the earth will mend,
When warmth returns to banish fright.

Awakening soon, the world will glow,
With flowers blooming in the sun's embrace.
But now we cherish the calming snow,
A fleeting moment in time and space.

Chasing Glistening Shadows

In the dusk, shadows play,
Whispering secrets of the day.
Glistening paths in twilight glow,
Leading where the heart might go.

Fleeting dreams on velvet air,
Echoes of laughter everywhere.
Footsteps soft on cobblestone,
Chasing shadows, we are not alone.

Stars adorn the velvet sea,
Guiding the souls who dare to be.
With each glance, a memory made,
In the dance of light that won't fade.

Beneath the veil of starlit skies,
Whispers of love in each sunrise.
We chase the glimmers, running free,
In the realm of what could be.

Holding tight to dreams unknown,
In every shadow, a truth is grown.
Together we find our way,
Chasing glistening shadows of the day.

Icy Echoes of the Night

The night wraps tight in crystal chill,
Whispers echo, clarity still.
Footfalls gentle on frosty ground,
Lost in the silence, no other sound.

Moonlit beams trace every line,
Shapes dance softly, so divine.
Icy breath mingles with the air,
In this world, nothing's rare.

Stars above, a distant glow,
Glinting softly, moving slow.
Each twinkle sings a lullaby,
In the stillness, spirits fly.

Winds whispering secrets so light,
Cold embraces in the night.
In the dark, a heart takes flight,
Finding warmth in icy might.

Through the shadows, we will tread,
With icy echoes, dreams are fed.
Each moment frozen, a fleeting grace,
In the night, we find our place.

Crystals Beneath the Moon

Underneath the silver light,
Crystals glimmer, pure and bright.
Each shard holds a tale to tell,
In the calm, we know it well.

Rippling waters reflect the glow,
Dancing softly, ever slow.
Nature's gems on gentle waves,
In their beauty, the spirit saves.

Moonlit paths of diamond dust,
In the night, we place our trust.
Crystals whisper ancient lore,
In their depths, we wander more.

Through the forest, warm embrace,
Finding solace in this space.
Echoes of dreams in every gleam,
Crystals glisten, weave the dream.

With the night as our cocoon,
We dance beneath the silent moon.
In the softest glow we find,
Crystals beneath, our hearts aligned.

Enchanted by the Chill

A breath of cold, the world transforms,
In winter's grasp, the silence warms.
Nature dons her frosty gown,
In this magic, we won't drown.

Glistening branches, pure as snow,
Invite the heart to dance and flow.
Every moment, a timeless thrill,
Together here, enchanted by the chill.

The night brings tales we long to share,
Secrets whispered in the air.
Stars beckon us in the dark,
As shadows weave their mystic spark.

In this stillness, laughter rings,
Creating joy that winter brings.
Holding hands, we find our way,
Enchanted by the chill, we stay.

Snowflakes twirl in spiraled dance,
In this beauty, we find our chance.
Wrapped in warmth, hearts together,
In the enchantment of the weather.

Wisps of Wonder in the Chill

The night air whispers soft and low,
As silver stars begin to glow.
Each breath a cloud, so pure and white,
Embraced by calm, we find delight.

The trees stand still in frosty grace,
A world transformed in winter's embrace.
With every step, the crunch resounds,
In nature's hush, true peace is found.

A glimmer of light on icy ground,
Where magic in the silence is found.
Wisps of wonder twirl and spin,
Drawing us closer, deep within.

The chill wraps round, a tender hug,
While moonlight dances, warm and snug.
In this serene, enchanted scene,
The heart finds joy, the soul feels free.

So let us roam where dreams take flight,
In wisps of wonder through the night.
Beneath the stars, in frost's embrace,
We savor winter's timeless grace.

A Tincture of Ice and Dream

In twilight's glow, a world stands still,
As shadows blend with winter's chill.
A tincture sweet, of ice and dream,
Where every moment shines and gleams.

The rivers sleep beneath their sheets,
Of glassy frost, where silence greets.
A whisper flows through frozen trees,
Serenading all the hidden pleas.

With every sigh, the night unfolds,
A tale of warmth in the bitter cold.
Lights twinkle softly, a distant song,
In this stillness, we all belong.

We chase the moon with hearts so light,
As dreams take shape in the starry night.
With every step, we weave a spell,
In this winter's heart, all is well.

So let us wander hand in hand,
Through realms of ice, so gently planned.
In a tincture of joy and gleam,
We find our truth, we find our dream.

The Allure of a Frostbitten Night

Under the glow of a silver dome,
The frost sings songs of a hidden home.
Each flake a gem, so pure and bright,
Captivating hearts on this magical night.

The crisp air bites, but oh, the thrill,
As shadows dance on the icy hill.
With every breath, there's life anew,
In the chill, we feel the view.

The stars above like diamonds shine,
In the grip of winter, our fates entwine.
A hush envelops, a sacred tune,
Luring us closer to the waiting moon.

The allure ignites with every glance,
As moonlight beckons us to dance.
With frost-kissed cheeks and laughter bright,
We celebrate the frostbitten night.

So take my hand, let's chase the frost,
In this dreamscape, we count the cost.
For in the allure of cold and dark,
We find the warmth, the secret spark.

The Secrets Hidden Beneath the Ice

Beneath the frozen, crystal veil,
Lie whispers of a timeless tale.
A world concealed in icy grace,
Where secrets hide, a sacred space.

The shadows dance in silent streams,
Unearthing echoes of forgotten dreams.
With every crack, the winter sighs,
Revealing truths to prying eyes.

A flicker of light beneath the chill,
Hints at magic, unseen yet still.
The stories woven in frosty lace,
Are waiting for a brave embrace.

So gather 'round, embrace the night,
Let's seek the beauty, the hidden light.
For in the depths of cold and clear,
The secrets whisper, drawing near.

Together we'll unveil each theme,
In the silent hush, as soft as dream.
The ice will yield, the past laid bare,
A tapestry of wonder in the air.

Snowbound Memories

Snowflakes dance upon the ground,
Softly swirling all around.
Children laugh in pure delight,
Creating magic in the white.

Footprints trace a story told,
Adventures in the winter's hold.
Fires crackle, warmth is near,
In these moments, all is clear.

Nights grow long with stars aglow,
Whispers caught in breezes slow.
Blankets wrap both heart and soul,
In winter's grasp, we feel whole.

Memories wrapped in frosty air,
Moments cherished, free of care.
As the world outside stands still,
We find comfort, warmth to fill.

Years may pass as seasons change,
But these memories feel no strange.
Each flake a kiss from skies above,
A timeless gift, a whispered love.

Crystalized Longing

A shimmer hangs in frosty air,
Dreams of warmth, we linger there.
Snowflakes fall, a tender sigh,
Wishes woven, whispered high.

Silent streets where shadows play,
Longing for the light of day.
Crystal shards reflect our gaze,
Yearning hearts in winter's maze.

Echoes of laughter from the past,
Lingering shadows, we hold fast.
Cold embraces, yet we yearn,
For the warmth that we discern.

Footsteps crunch on powdery ground,
In this stillness, love is found.
Each breath visible in the chill,
Our hearts steady, dreams fulfill.

Carried forth on winter's breeze,
In the hush, we find our peace.
Crystalized wishes twinkle bright,
Guiding us through the longest night.

Iced Reveries

Through icy panes, the world turns white,
Dreams unfold in soft moonlight.
Frozen whispers kiss the air,
A ballet of the lost and rare.

Memories dance in winter's grip,
Even time feels like a trip.
Visions clear as crystal skies,
Holding truths in silent sighs.

A tapestry of frost and cold,
Stories of the brave and bold.
Darkness swirled with hints of light,
In frozen realms, we take flight.

Underneath the blanket deep,
Sensations wake from restful sleep.
Iced reveries that we explore,
In this winter, we want more.

Let the chill inspire a dream,
In quietness, we find our theme.
A world transformed, serene and still,
Embraced by winter's tender thrill.

Whispers of Winter's Veil

Underneath a silver sky,
Gentle sighs of winter lie.
A whisper floats on frosty air,
Promises of warmth we share.

Glistened trees, a tranquil sight,
Nature wrapped in purest white.
Echoes of a world transformed,
In this stillness, we feel warmed.

Footsteps lead through falling snow,
Every step a tale to sow.
In the silence, peace descends,
Winter's magic never ends.

Stars adorn the velvet night,
Guiding dreams with tender light.
Winds of change, softly prevail,
Carrying whispers, winter's veil.

Together wrapped in flurries deep,
In the chill, our hearts we keep.
As seasons shift, and snowflakes melt,
From winter's grasp, true love is felt.

A Chill's Tender Caress

A breeze drifts soft and low,
Kissing cheeks with icy grace,
It whispers secrets as it goes,
Each flake a gentle embrace.

The trees stand still in quiet awe,
Assigned to dance without a sound,
Their branches bare, yet so much lore,
In every crystal, beauty found.

A world transformed in silver light,
Each shimmer holds a fleeting dream,
The air alight with pure delight,
In wonder, all the spirits gleam.

With every gust, the calmness brews,
A chilly tale unfolds anew,
Nature's breath in tranquil hues,
With every pulse, our hearts renew.

So let us walk this frozen night,
Through shadows cast by the moon's glow,
In hush we find a soft respite,
In a chill's tender caress, we flow.

Whispers of the Crystal Garden

Beneath the frost, a secret stirs,
A garden draped in shimmering light,
Each petal whispers through the firs,
In silence, magic takes its flight.

The moonlight bathes the world in gold,
Where starlit dreams begin to dance,
With every breath, the night unfolds,
In nature's soft and sweet romance.

Glistening paths weave through the trees,
The chill sings softly in the air,
While secrets flow upon the breeze,
Each moment, a gentle prayer.

The frost, like jewels, adorns the ground,
Embracing every earthly thing,
And in this hush, we feel the sound,
Of winter's heart, a tender spring.

Awake the night with dreams anew,
In whispers of the crystal air,
Together let us wander through,
A garden filled with silver flair.

Subdued Colors of Winter's Canvas

A palette draped in muted tones,
Where earth and sky find soft repose,
Beneath the chill, the quiet moans,
Of nature weaving tales in prose.

The landscape holds its breath in still,
Yet colors linger, shy and bold,
In subtle hues, the heart does fill,
With warmth against the winter's cold.

Each branch a brushstroke, pure and fine,
With frost-kissed tips, a tender touch,
The canvas speaks in whispered lines,
Of beauty resting, felt so much.

In softest grays and gentle blues,
The world becomes a softened dream,
A lullaby the season brews,
In silence, love's sweet, quiet beam.

So wander on this painted path,
Embrace the stillness of the morn,
In subdued colors, feel the wrath,
Turn into peace where art is born.

Luminous Paths through the Snow

The stars above begin to glow,
As twilight fades and shadows creep,
We walk upon the quilted snow,
In silence, where the world is deep.

Each step a crunch, a fleeting sound,
Beneath the moon's soft silver veil,
With every breath, joy can be found,
In pathways bright, our hearts set sail.

Luminous trails in winter's night,
Guide us through the frosted scene,
With every sparkle, pure delight,
A gentle peace where we have been.

The trees stand tall, adorned in white,
Their branches draped with crystal threads,
In this stillness, love takes flight,
As dreams and hopes are softly fed.

So let us roam these paths aglow,
Where winter's beauty whispers low,
With wonders wrapped in askew flow,
In luminous paths through the snow.

Threads of Frost and Fantasy

In the realm where dreams take flight,
Spins the loom of the frosty night.
Glimmers of magic in swirling air,
Whispers of wonder with each chilling stare.

Each thread woven with care and grace,
A tapestry bright, a delicate lace.
Frosty patterns, a dance in the dark,
Every sparkle igniting a spark.

From the depths of winter's embrace,
To the heart of a dreamer's chase.
Weaving tales where hopes intertwine,
In a world where the stars brightly shine.

The frost carries secrets from days of old,
Stories of magic forever told.
In the silence of night, the whispers flow,
Threads of fantasy gleaned in the snow.

Embers of twilight, vivid and bold,
Glistening tales of silver and gold.
In this landscape, our hearts can soar,
Threads of frost weave forevermore.

Shimmering Wishes on Cold Winds

Beneath the vast and starry sky,
Wishes take flight, the night winds sigh.
Each shimmering spark a silent plea,
Carried afar like a whispered decree.

Cold winds dance with the breath of fate,
Carving dreams on the heart's open gate.
In the shadows of night where wishes gleam,
Reality bends to a gentle dream.

Snowflakes twirl like little sighs,
An echo of hopes that softly rise.
As the chill weaves its melodic tune,
Wishes shimmer beneath the moon.

Each breath of frost, a promise concealed,
A secret of joys that winter revealed.
Let the cold winds carry your dreams far,
Shimmering bright like a distant star.

In the tranquil hush of the winter night,
Shimmering wishes take wing in flight.
Let your heart sing in the stillness of gray,
As cold winds guide you on your way.

Lullabies of a Snowy Dawn

In the stillness of dawn, snowflakes fall,
Whispering dreams, a soft, sweet call.
The world is hushed, blanketed white,
Lullabies murmur in the pale light.

Each flake a note in a gentle song,
Flowing together, where hearts belong.
Under the warmth of the breaking day,
Lullabies beckon, inviting to stay.

The quiet of morning, pure and serene,
Painting the world in glistening sheen.
Wrapped in warmth, by the fire's glow,
Tales of the winter softly flow.

Whispers of magic float on the breeze,
Carried on air with effortless ease.
In this moment, peace reigns profound,
As lullabies sing in the snowy dawn.

Embrace the promise of a new day,
As dreams awaken and gently sway.
In the arms of winter, love will remain,
Lullabies echo through joy and pain.

Glacial Encounters of the Heart

In the chill of love's icy embrace,
Hearts unfurl in a silent space.
Frosted connections, both tender and true,
Glacial encounters, a dance when anew.

Eyes like frost, shining so bright,
Capturing warmth in the heart of night.
Each glance a promise, each touch a spark,
In the depths of winter, ignite the dark.

Beneath the surface, the currents flow,
Where glacial rivers through heartbeats grow.
Every heartbeat, a tale to share,
In the winter's chill, a love laid bare.

Time stands still in the soft, white snow,
Gathering moments in the night's quiet glow.
Each breath, an echo of feelings released,
In glacial encounters, love finds its peace.

As the world melts in the warmth of your gaze,
Hearts thaw in the sun's tender rays.
In this winter wonder, let love be the art,
Crafted by glacial encounters of the heart.

Glittering Dreams

In twilight's hush, the stars appear,
Whispers of hope, drawing near.
A tapestry woven in silver light,
Guiding lost souls through the night.

In waking hours, they softly gleam,
Carving paths through every dream.
Colors splash in cosmic dance,
Every heartbeat, a chance to prance.

With every breath, the visions grow,
Casting shadows, soft and low.
In laughter's joy, in silence deep,
The universe cradles dreams we keep.

With glimmering thoughts and fervent sighs,
We chase the light that never dies.
In sparkling night, our spirits soar,
In glittering dreams, we seek for more.

So rise with the dawn, embrace the fire,
With every step, let your heart aspire.
The world is vast, with wonders found,
In glittering dreams, we are unbound.

Serene Chill

A blanket of snow wraps the ground,
In stillness, only whispers sound.
Breath turns to mist, in the frosty air,
Nature gathers, a moment rare.

The trees stand tall, draped in white,
Moonlight gleams, a guiding light.
Crystals form on every breath,
In this embrace, we dance with death.

Stars twinkle bright in the deep blue sky,
Under the chill, the spirits fly.
A tranquil hush settles all around,
In this winter, peace is found.

Glistening ice on every branch,
Inviting hearts to take a chance.
In frozen beauty, moments cease,
A serene chill brings quiet peace.

So let us wander, hand in hand,
Through this winter wonderland.
In the serene chill, we'll find our way,
With whispers of love in skies of gray.

Celestial Frost

Beneath the dome of the countless stars,
A soft reminder of who we are.
Celestial frost coats hopes anew,
Painting dreams in icy hue.

Galaxies swirl in a dance divine,
Every heartbeat, a radiant sign.
In the night sky, a story unfolds,
Of forgotten legends and dreams retold.

The moon hangs low, a silver gaze,
Guiding wanderers through the haze.
In shimmering lights, the cosmos hums,
With every twinkle, our spirit comes.

Awake in the stillness, we soar and glide,
Embracing the frost, where wonders abide.
Through shimmering silence, we seek our fate,
In celestial paths, we learn to wait.

So reach for the stars, let your spirit fly,
In the grasp of frost, we touch the sky.
With dreams as our map, we'll never be lost,
Together we journey through celestial frost.

Glistening Horizons

At dawn's first light, the world awakes,
With colors bright as the earth it shakes.
A canvas painted, bold and wide,
Glistening horizons, where dreams reside.

Each wave of the ocean, a tale to tell,
In whispers of breezes, we find our spell.
Mountains rise high, kissed by the sun,
In golden hues, our lives begun.

Infinite skies stretch far and near,
With every heartbeat, hopes appear.
In every step, a new sunbeams,
Chasing shadows, igniting dreams.

The pathways gleam, with promise bright,
Leading us forward into the light.
With every breath, we grasp the day,
In glistening horizons, we find our way.

So take a moment, breathe it in,
Let the adventure of life begin.
In this journey, our hearts will guide,
To glistening horizons, where dreams abide.

Distant Icicles

Beneath the winter's breath, they sway,
Crystal daggers in disarray.
They catch the light, a fleeting dance,
In the silence, they hold their stance.

Glimmers of cold in twilight's hue,
Whispers of frost, a chilling view.
The world around, a frozen still,
Nature's art, a serene thrill.

Hanging gently from the roof's edge,
Each one tells a tale, a pledge.
Of seasons past, and winter's song,
In their beauty, we all belong.

As sunlight breaks, they start to weep,
Droplets falling, secrets deep.
A fleeting moment, soon to fade,
Yet in their shine, memories made.

Distant icicles, a sight to behold,
Stories etched in glimmers bold.
As the days warm, they bid adieu,
Leaving whispers of winter's view.

Shivery Reveries

In the dawn's gentle embrace,
Frosty whispers guide the chase.
Dreams wrapped in a shivering coat,
Drifting softly, like a lonely boat.

Moonlit nights bring tales untold,
In shivery dreams, our hearts unfold.
We wander through the misty dark,
Seeking solace, a tiny spark.

Bare branches tremble, shadows creep,
While the world lies fast asleep.
In reveries born from the night,
We weave our hopes, fragile and light.

A dance of flurries, soft and slow,
In shivery pulses, feelings flow.
Through icy streets, we find our way,
Holding close what dreams convey.

Awake we rise, to morning's glow,
With echoes of night, our thoughts in tow.
And as the sun warms the frost away,
Shivery reveries here to stay.

Celestial Dew

Morning breaks with a tender sigh,
Celestial drops from the sky.
Sparkling gems on blades of green,
Nature's whisper, fresh and clean.

Each droplet holds a starry night,
Glimmering softly in the light.
A world reborn, kissed by grace,
In dew's embrace, we find our place.

They glisten bright as the day begins,
Holding secrets of where it spins.
A fleeting moment, sweet and true,
In each small orb, a cosmic view.

As sun climbs high, they slowly fade,
Leaving trails where dreams once played.
Yet memories linger, fresh and new,
In the heart, celestial dew.

Nature's promise, a cycle spun,
With every dawn, a chance begun.
We'll chase the light, the skies so blue,
To dance beneath the celestial dew.

Luminous Glint

In the stillness of the night,
Stars awaken, soft and bright.
A luminous glint, a written tale,
Guiding dreams on a silken trail.

They twinkle high, like distant eyes,
Winking gently from the skies.
A canvas dark, with sparkles bold,
Secrets woven, the universe told.

Through whispered winds, they softly hum,
Echoing where the heartbeats drum.
In the shadows, they dance and play,
Fading whispers of the day.

A nightingale sings beneath their glow,
In melodies where feelings flow.
With every glint, a wish takes flight,
In the vastness of starry night.

So when the world seems tough and grim,
Let the luminous glint not dim.
For each star holds a wish within,
A promise waiting for you to begin.

The Dance of Icy Breath

In the hush of night, stars gleam bright,
Whispers of winter take their flight.
Moonlight glistens on the frozen ground,
A symphony of silence, no other sound.

The air is crisp, with a biting chill,
Nature awakens, as time stands still.
The branches sway, like dancers so free,
In this frosty ballet, just you and me.

Snowflakes twirl in a graceful waltz,
Each unique, yet no one faults.
They gather in patterns, soft and light,
Creating a canvas, pure and white.

With every breath, the icy air glows,
Painting the world in delicate flows.
A fleeting moment, forever to keep,
As in this dance, we dream and leap.

The night draws on, but we won't part,
This dance of icy breath warms the heart.
So let us sway, through the chill and frost,
In this winter's breath, never lost.

Frost-kissed Fantasies at Dawn

Soft light breaks, as the night does yield,
Frost-kissed dreams across the field.
Whispers of dawn awaken the trees,
A magical moment, wrapped in a breeze.

In the golden glow, shadows softly fade,
Dewdrops sparkle, a shimmering parade.
Each blade of grass, with diamonds adorned,
Nature's treasure, in silence, is born.

Birds start to chirp, a sweet serenade,
Echoes of life in this frosty glade.
The world stirs anew, with colors so bright,
Frost-kissed fantasies, in morning light.

As sunlight dances on the icy sheen,
Awakening dreams, from the night so serene.
Each moment whispers, "Just breathe and be,"
In this frosty wonder, together, we see.

The day unfolds, with a gentle embrace,
Frost-kissed visions, in time and space.
Let's wander through shadows and beams of dawn,
Embracing the magic, till the light is gone.

Twilight Serenade in the Snow

In twilight's glow, the world turns to grey,
The snow begins to softly sway.
Whispers of winter fill the falling night,
A serenade sung in shimmering light.

Silence envelops the chilly ground,
Footprints echo, a ghostly sound.
Each flake that falls, a note on the air,
Creating a harmony, flawless and rare.

The trees stand tall, wearing coats of white,
As stars twinkle softly, blinking in the night.
A blanket of snow, so pure and divine,
Holding our dreams, as our hearts entwine.

As the moon rises, it bathes us in glow,
Illuminating paths where the cold winds blow.
In this twilight serenade, we feel so free,
Embracing the magic of you and me.

The night is alive, with whispers untold,
A story of winter, in warmth we hold.
With each gentle sigh, we wander this land,
In twilight's embrace, together we stand.

Ephemeral Whispers of the Frozen

In the stillness, a breath, a sigh,
Ephemeral whispers, floating by.
Frosty tendrils wrap the trees,
A delicate dance in the frigid breeze.

Layers of crystals coat the ground,
Each step we take is a muffled sound.
Voices of winter call us to see,
Nature's still beauty, wild and free.

Moonlight cascades on the icy stream,
Reflecting the night, like a fleeting dream.
Shadows flicker as stars wane,
In this frozen world, we lose all pain.

Yet time is fleeting, then like the dawn,
These whispers will fade; we carry on.
But in this moment, let's not let go,
Embrace the silence, let love overflow.

As the night deepens, we savor the thrill,
Of ephemeral whispers, both gentle and still.
A fleeting sigh, as we wrap in the cold,
Hold tight to this magic, more precious than gold.

Dreams Woven in Winter Light

In quiet corners, shadows play,
As whispers dance in frosty air,
The world adorned in silver sway,
We weave our dreams without a care.

The dawn arrives, a gentle hue,
With glimmering starlight all around,
Each thought a thread, each breath anew,
In winter's grasp, our hearts unbound.

Beneath the frost, the secrets sleep,
Awakening with the morning's glare,
In every sigh, our hopes we keep,
As fleeting moments linger there.

Through snowy fields, we wander wide,
Each footprint tells a tale of grace,
With winter's chill, we walk with pride,
Embracing light in this cold space.

So let us stitch the dreams we share,
With laughter bright and love so bright,
In winter's warmth, we banish care,
And revel in this woven light.

The Glow of Crystal Shards

A tapestry of shards appears,
As sunlight weaves through frozen trees,
Each glint a memory that cheers,
A symphony of winter's keys.

In crystalline, the world transformed,
With colors bright, a stunning sight,
Each sparkle glows, each heart is warmed,
As nature sings in pure delight.

The quiet hush, the gentle breeze,
Carried on clouds of snowy white,
In every breath, the air's at ease,
While dreams reflect in crystal light.

So let us roam in frosty fields,
Among the glimmers, hand in hand,
Where every moment softly yields,
A fragile beauty, bright and grand.

With laughter ringing through the air,
We seize the day, our spirits soar,
In the glow of shards, love we share,
As winter's magic opens door.

Clouded Thoughts on a Snowy Evening

A quiet night, the snowflakes fall,
With thoughts adrift like winter's haze,
In clouds of white, I feel it all,
As memories dance through vague arrays.

The world outside in fragile peace,
Each flake a whisper drawn from dreams,
In this stillness, thoughts release,
As cold embraces softly gleams.

The fireplace crackles, shadows play,
While echoes of the day recede,
In winter's arms, we drift away,
With every moment, hearts are freed.

The silver moonlight paints the sky,
A tapestry of gentle white,
In cloudy thoughts, I pause and sigh,
Embracing all this tranquil night.

As night unfolds, a canvas bare,
I find my peace amidst the snow,
In quiet minds, our dreams lay bare,
While winter's breath—soft winds that blow.

Embracing the Frozen Stillness

In frozen stillness, silence reigns,
Each moment carved in icy time,
The world holds breath, the heart regains,
A pulse beneath the winter's rhyme.

The trees adorned in crystal lace,
Stand sentinel 'neath canopy,
In nature's arms, we find our place,
A refuge sweet, a tapestry.

The stars above, so sharp and bright,
Glimmer like dreams in velvet skies,
Each twinkle speaks of hope's true light,
A promise held where beauty lies.

Wrapped in the warmth of love's embrace,
We celebrate this quiet time,
Where frozen stillness finds its grace,
And whispers echo, soft as chime.

So let us dance in winter's glow,
In rhythms rich with joy and peace,
With every step, our spirits flow,
Embracing life, our hearts increase.

Icy Whispers

In the stillness, secrets sigh,
Frosty winds begin to cry.
Moonlit paths of silver gleam,
Echoes of a frozen dream.

Snowflakes dance on weary trees,
Whispers ride the evening breeze.
Shadows stretch, embracing night,
Stars above, so cold, so bright.

Silence wraps the world in white,
Chilling tales of winter's plight.
Footsteps lost in powdered snow,
Mirrored lakes with hearts aglow.

Each breath forms a misty cloud,
Nature's magic, quiet, loud.
Frosty branches softly bend,
In the night, the dreamers send.

A hush blankets the earth so deep,
Icy whispers, secrets keep.
Underneath the starlit skies,
Winter speaks while silence lies.

Shimmering Visions

In the twilight, dreams arise,
Colors dance, a sweet surprise.
Golden hues and silver mist,
Painting worlds that can't be missed.

Mountains glow with sunset fire,
Whispers soft, my heart's desire.
Waves of light in every fold,
Mysteries in shades of gold.

Through the branches, light breaks free,
Casting wonders for us to see.
Moments glow, then slip away,
Shimmering visions, night and day.

Every glance, a fleeting chance,
Colors woven in a dance.
Magic lives in every beam,
Life unfolds like a vivid dream.

With each heartbeat, visions soar,
Boundless light forevermore.
In the stillness, take your flight,
Shimmer brightly against the night.

Chilled Fantasies

Beneath the frost, the fantasies flow,
Winds of wonder, soft and low.
Buried dreams in snowy beds,
Whispered thoughts in winter threads.

Icicles hang, like dreams on a thread,
Frosted visions inside my head.
Hushed reflections on frozen lakes,
Chilled fantasies, the heart awakes.

Every flake a story told,
Crystal castles, brave and bold.
In the quiet, soft and bright,
Chilled adventures, pure delight.

Through the haze of winter's grip,
Magic dances, spirits flip.
Silent echoes softly call,
Chilled fantasies that bind us all.

In this realm of ice and light,
Every heartbeat feels so right.
Let the dreams take hold and sway,
Chilled fantasies will find their way.

Crystal Lullabies

Under the stars, a lullaby sings,
Wrapped in warmth, the spirit clings.
Crystal notes on the cool night air,
Whispers of love beyond compare.

Gentle breezes brush my face,
In their arms, I find my place.
Softly, softly, the moments weave,
Crystal dreams that we believe.

Each melody a tender kiss,
Filling the night with soothing bliss.
In the silence, hearts align,
Crystal lullabies, so divine.

Time stands still in this embrace,
Hearts ignite with every trace.
Through the night, the songs will flow,
Guiding us where love will grow.

As dawn approaches, soft and bright,
Crystal dreams yield to the light.
But in our hearts, they'll softly lie,
Forever cherished, like the sky.

Hallowed Frost

In the hush of winter's breath,
Snowflakes dance, a silent death.
Glistening trees in white embrace,
Nature wears a frosty lace.

Footprints trace a ghostly path,
Echoing the quiet math.
In the moonlight's frozen glow,
Whispers of the night bestow.

Blankets wrap the world in dreams,
Starlit skies dance with moonbeams.
Crystals form on window panes,
Hallowed whispers in the lanes.

Fires crackle in cozy nooks,
While the world reads frozen books.
Time stands still, a fleeting pause,
In a realm where magic draws.

As dawn breaks with gentle hues,
Frosty fields like woven blues.
In the heart of winter's reign,
Hallowed frost shall ever reign.

Twilight Whispers

Underneath the fading light,
Shadows stretch into the night.
Stars emerge, a twinkling sea,
Whispers soft as dreams can be.

Crisp air carries tales afar,
Echoes of the evening star.
Luna casts her silver tide,
Guiding hearts where love can hide.

Colors blend, a canvas bright,
Twilight wraps the day in night.
Birds retreat with songs of gold,
Mysteries of dusk unfold.

In the stillness, secrets sigh,
Breath of night, a gentle lie.
Worlds collide in soft embrace,
Timeless moments leave no trace.

As the hours begin to wane,
Dreamers stroll through soft terrain.
Twilight's whispers beckon near,
In the silence, hearts will clear.

Subzero Visions

Frosted panes and icy hues,
Capturing the morning dews.
Landscapes draped in chilly mist,
Where dreams and reality twist.

Glistening candles burn so bright,
Flickering in the velvet night.
Snowflakes fall like whispered tales,
Carrying the winter gales.

In the stillness, time runs slow,
Frozen lakes with secrets glow.
Mirrored skies in icy frames,
Subzero visions, wild games.

Windswept paths lead far away,
Tracing stories night and day.
With each breath, the magic swirls,
Dancing light in winter's pearls.

As the night begins to fade,
Morning light, a soft cascade.
Subzero visions linger on,
In the hearts of those who dawn.

Crystalline Delusions

In a realm where worlds collide,
Crystalline dreams cannot hide.
Shimmering thoughts like glassy spheres,
Reflecting all our hopes and fears.

Mocking shadows play their game,
Illusions set the soul aflame.
Frozen laughter fills the air,
Capturing the heart's despair.

Whispers weave through icy trees,
Telling tales in the chilly breeze.
Gems of wisdom, frozen bright,
Sparkling softly in the night.

In the dance of shards and rays,
Light confesses in subtle ways.
Within the crystal's gentle gleam,
Lie the secrets of a dream.

As dawn breaks, the visions fade,
Leaving echoes softly laid.
Crystalline delusions wane,
Yet their beauty will remain.

Wistful Icescapes

Glistening fields of frosted dreams,
Beneath the sky, where silence gleams.
Whispers of winter in the night,
Moonlit shadows bathe in white.

Tales of snowflakes dance on air,
Each one unique, beyond compare.
Gentle breezes, soft and low,
Time stands still, frozen aglow.

Stillness awakens hearts to muse,
In the chill, the world we choose.
Paths of crystal, etched in grace,
In this realm, we find our place.

Sparkling rivers, winding slow,
Hushed reflections, gentle flow.
Nature's canvas, painted bright,
Whispers echo through the night.

Wistful dreams in icy hues,
A world embraced in frosty blues.
In this moment, peace prevails,
As winter's breath weaves silent tales.

Slumbering Chill

In the quiet of a winter's sigh,
Softly blankets drift and fly.
Trees adorned in purest white,
Guard the secrets of the night.

Endless skies in deepening gray,
Wrap the earth in muted play.
Dancing snowflakes on the breeze,
Cold embraces, hearts at ease.

Voices faint, like distant dreams,
Echo softly in the streams.
Frosted whispers glide along,
A lullaby, a winter song.

In the slumber of the snow,
Time is gentle, movements slow.
Warmth within the frigid air,
Finding solace everywhere.

Chill descends with tender grace,
Crystals form in nature's space.
Wrapped in layers, warmth we feel,
As we drift in winter's seal.

Veils of Winter

A tapestry of white unfurls,
Blanketing the quiet world.
Each breath a cloud, the air so still,
Time is wrapped in winter's chill.

Tendrils of frost on windows trace,
Nature's lace, a soft embrace.
Branches bow with heavy crowns,
While solitude in beauty drowns.

Horizon stretches, pale and wide,
Chasing shadows that softly hide.
A veil of silence sweeps the ground,
With every whisper, peace is found.

Snowflakes twirl like fleeting thoughts,
Softly landing, worlds they wrought.
Winds caress, a soothing song,
In this realm we all belong.

Veils of winter, gently spun,
Breathe life into what's come undone.
In the stillness, hearts take flight,
Woven dreams in the softest light.

Frozen Whimsy

Upon the lake, a crystal sheen,
Where dreams become what once has been.
Laughter echoes, children play,
In a world of white ballet.

Icicles hang like jeweled threads,
The earth adorned with snowy beds.
Footprints lead to hidden trails,
Chasing after winter gales.

Glimmering worlds of ice and snow,
In every corner, magic flows.
Imagination takes its flight,
In frozen whims beneath starlight.

Frosted whispers swirl and twine,
A dance of joy so sweet, divine.
With every flake, a tale is spun,
In the heart where dreams are won.

Frozen whimsy, a fleeting chance,
To lose ourselves in winter's dance.
As summers fade and chill descends,
The spirit of winter gently blends.

Fragments of Glittering Snow

Frosted whispers kiss the ground,
Dancing flakes in silence found.
Each a jewel, pure and bright,
Sparkling softly in the night.

They swirl and twirl, a fleeting grace,
Nature's art in a soft embrace.
Glistening paths we gently trace,
Lost in beauty, time's sweet chase.

Underneath the moon's soft glow,
World transformed by winter's show.
In the stillness, dreams awake,
Heartfelt wishes, hopes we make.

Every flake a tale to weave,
Moments cherished, hearts believe.
In this realm where silence reigns,
Joy and wonder fill our veins.

Fragments gather, drifting slow,
Covering all in purest snow.
A tapestry, a world anew,
Nature's canvas, vast and true.

In the Heart of the Winter's Grip

Cold winds whisper through the trees,
Wrapped in layers, we feel the freeze.
Each breath forms a cloud so bright,
In the heart of winter's night.

Shadows dance on frozen ground,
A symphony of silence found.
Stars above, a distant song,
In this chill, we all belong.

The world is hushed, the fire glows,
Where the river quietly flows.
Muffled steps on blankets white,
In the depth of winter's night.

With every flake, a story spun,
Crafting dreams as they are done.
In the grip of icy grace,
We find warmth in this embrace.

Hearts ignite with fervent spark,
Guided by the winter's dark.
Cocoa steams in frosted air,
Each moment savored, offered prayer.

The Shimmer of Subtle Magic

Underneath the silver moon,
Softly glimmers, winter's tune.
Nature hums a gentle refrain,
Whispers weave our dreams again.

Frosted branches paint the trees,
Quiet magic in the breeze.
Each step taken, secrets shared,
In the stillness, souls are bared.

Glimmers dance upon the lake,
As the night begins to wake.
In their shimmer, stories lie,
Whispered to the velvet sky.

Moments flicker, caught in time,
Subtle magic, pure and sublime.
As we roam through starry night,
Heartbeats echo, pure delight.

In the shadows, dreams ignite,
Sparkling under soft moonlight.
With each breath, the world feels whole,
In this magic, find your soul.

Celestial Frost in Quiet Moments

Morning breaks with gentle light,
Frosted whispers, pure and bright.
Each blade glistens with a grace,
Softly held in winter's embrace.

Time stands still on snowy hills,
Nature whispering, silence fills.
Celestial beauty starts to wake,
Icy echoes, stillness take.

Crystals forming, nature's lace,
Sparkling softly, dreams we chase.
In each breath, the chill brings peace,
In these moments, worries cease.

The world transforms as shadows flee,
Frosty breath, a symphony.
In their hush, life finds its beat,
Winter's magic, oh so sweet.

As we wander through this dream,
Time unravels, thoughts redeem.
In the frost, a quiet song,
Melodies where we belong.

Enchanted Chill

In twilight's grasp, a shimmering glow,
Soft whispers dance in the winter's flow.
The trees stand tall, with snowflakes spun,
A world aglow, where dreams are spun.

Moonlit shadows, a serene delight,
Painting the night with silver light.
Each breath a cloud, crisp in the air,
A heart's embrace, in the stillness, rare.

Secrets held in the icy breeze,
Where nature hums with gentle ease.
Footprints trace tales of wonder's flight,
In the enchanted chill of the night.

Stars awaken, in blankets of white,
Casting their wishes, a dazzling sight.
Hope sparkles, like frost on a leaf,
In moments stilled, we find belief.

Wrapped in wonder, we pause and dream,
The world transformed, a glistening theme.
In enchanted chill, our spirits soar,
Forever held in winter's door.

Ethereal Slumbers

Beneath the stars, where silence reigns,
The night embraces, with gentle chains.
Draped in dreams, the world lies still,
Wrapped in warmth, beneath the hill.

Whispers of night, a soothing sigh,
In ethereal slumbers, the spirits fly.
The moon, a guardian, watches close,
A serene vigil, for dreams engrossed.

Waves of rest, caress the mind,
In the hush of night, solace we find.
Clouds of slumber, soft and light,
Guide us gently, into the night.

Stars like lanterns, twinkle above,
Casting their glow on the dreams we love.
Embraced in shadows, fears take flight,
In the cradle of peace, all feels right.

Through night's embrace, we drift and flow,
Journeying where the heart would go.
In ethereal slumbers, lost in grace,
In the quietude, we find our place.

Frost-Flecked Yearnings

When winter weaves its frosty lace,
A chill descends, a soft embrace.
Frost flecked dreams, in crystal white,
Sparkle and shimmer in the night.

Breath hangs heavy, in the cool air,
Longing whispers, a silent prayer.
Through the stillness, hopes take wing,
In the frost's glow, our hearts can sing.

Moments captured in glistening frost,
In the stillness, we find what's lost.
Beneath the blanket of winter's sigh,
Yearnings awaken, in dreams that fly.

The shimmer fades, like echoes past,
Yet in the chill, our wishes last.
For every flake that falls and swirls,
Holds a promise, as time unfurls.

In frost-flecked yearnings, we feel alive,
As nature's beauty helps us thrive.
Wrapped in magic, our spirits soar,
In winter's arms, we seek for more.

Aetherial Frost

In realms where winter's whispers blend,
Aetherial frost, on dreams descend.
Each crystal branch tells tales untold,
Of love and loss, in the cold.

Echoes linger in the frozen air,
A tender silence, beyond compare.
Snowflakes flutter, like thoughts on breeze,
Laced with memories, bringing ease.

Waking the world from midday's sleep,
In frosty shrouds, the secrets keep.
Beneath the white, the earth does sigh,
Under a canvas, vast and high.

Aetherial dance of the moon's embrace,
Sweeping shadows that time can't erase.
The chill brings clarity, in its hold,
A serenity sweet, a story bold.

Wrapped in the charm of a quiet night,
Aetherial frost fills hearts with light.
In every flake, a wish we cast,
In winter's beauty, we find our past.

Echoes from an Icy Horizon

Whispers of winter in the breeze,
Silent echoes dance through the trees.
Footsteps follow where shadows meet,
Cold breaths linger beneath my feet.

Glistening crystals catch the light,
A world transformed, pure and bright.
Frozen dreams float on the air,
Each heartbeat a quiet prayer.

Shadows stretch in the fading day,
Nature's canvas, a wondrous display.
Softly we glide on a breath of frost,
In this realm, we find what's lost.

The horizon beckons, grand and wide,
A tranquil journey, let's glide.
Underneath skies so vast, serene,
In frozen landscapes, we glean.

Whispers of time linger around,
In icy silence, truths are found.
Echoes from an icy expanse,
We find ourselves in winter's dance.

Enigma of the Glistening White

In the hush of winter's grace,
A veil of white, an endless space.
Mysterious realms wrapped in frost,
In their beauty, we are engrossed.

Shapes morph gently in the glow,
A subtle dance, a quiet show.
Shimmering fields stretch far and near,
In every corner, magic here.

Footprints trace a story untold,
In the mysteries that winter holds.
Each flake unique, a fleeting tale,
In this wonder, we shall prevail.

Moonlight bathes the world in peace,
The chill brings whispers of release.
Stars above twinkle in delight,
An enigma of the glistening white.

With every sigh, the cold air bites,
In its embrace, we find our heights.
Wrapped in dreams of purest snow,
The heart finds warmth in winter's glow.

Chilly Reveries on Starry Nights

Underneath the vast, dark sky,
Stars awaken, twinkling high.
Each one a wish, a distant song,
In chilly reveries, we belong.

Frozen whispers fill the air,
A symphony of dreams laid bare.
The night unfolds its glistening sheet,
Where frost and wonder gently meet.

Moonlight dances on silvered fields,
Nature's magic silently yields.
In the stillness, hearts ignite,
Chasing shadows in the night.

Moments linger, time stands still,
With every breath, we feel the thrill.
In the cool embrace of the night,
We lose ourselves, no need for light.

As the stars spin tales of yore,
Our spirits rise, we long for more.
In chilly reveries, we entwine,
Forever captured, yours and mine.

Palette of Ice and Wonder

A canvas drawn in shades of blue,
Icicles glisten, a frosty hue.
Nature paints with every breath,
A palette that hints at life and death.

Soft whispers echo through the night,
In shadows warm, where spirits light.
Colors dance in a cool embrace,
An artful glimpse of time and space.

Frosted branches bend with grace,
Each crystal crafted, a delicate trace.
Beneath the surface, secrets bloom,
In icy depths, away from gloom.

Wonders hidden in the cold,
Stories of the brave and bold.
With each stroke of winter's hand,
In this beauty, we understand.

A symphony of white and light,
In the depths of the starry night.
This magic, a fleeting treasure,
A palette of ice that we measure.

Milton Keynes UK
Ingram Content Group UK Ltd.
UKHW021046031224
452078UK00010B/599

9 789916 797